Attract Birds to Your Garden

By Jeanne Grunert

Attract Birds to Your Garden

By Jeanne Grunert

Many thanks to Mr. Krausankas for permission to use his photography on the cover of this book.

Disclaimer

ISBN-13: 978-1502554574

Contents

Introduction: Reasons to Attract Birds Year Round

Who hasn't noticed a flock of birds soaring across the sky? Perhaps a bright red bird caught your eye one morning and you wondered what it was. Or maybe you visited a neighbor's house in high summer and were amused by the antics of hummingbirds dancing around a nectar feeder.

Welcome to *Attracting Birds to Your Garden*, a beginner's guide to attracting, feeding, and enjoying wild birds. According to some sources, close to 82 million people[i] in the United States feed wild birds; that's about 27% of the population. Attracting, feeding and watching wild birds provide hours of enjoyment for every member of the family, from the oldest to the youngest. For many people, getting to know the wild birds in their backyard, whether it's an urban lot or a rural field, is the gateway to learning more about the environment, conservation, and the natural world.

The earliest recorded instance of people feeding the birds is the story of St. Serf of Fife, a monk living in sixth century Europe. He's rumored to have tamed a wild robin by feeding it. It's likely, though, that throughout history mankind has fed wild birds. There's a good reason for it.

Organic Insect Control

Although you may immediately think of bird seed when you hear terms such as feeding the birds, birds eat a wide variety of foods, including insects. A study in the United Kingdom[ii] indicated that feeding birds attracts many more birds to the backyard garden. Such birds in turn take up residence nearby and eat insects, including the 'bad' bugs that plague the backyard gardener. Establishing friendships with wild birds by providing them with food, water and shelter suited to their needs encourages colonies to take up residence nearby. In exchange for your gifts, such birds give back generously by gobbling up insects and keeping the insect population down. If you use organic gardening methods, the insects they eat won't pass on pesticides and chemicals that can damage the birds or their eggs. You'll support nature's best pest control methods.

Cultivating Environment Awareness

It's amazing how many people grow up unaware of the vast diversity of flora and fauna right in their own backyards. The most urban environment may house pigeons and hawks, sparrows and grackles, and hundreds more species. Suburban yards offer food and shelter to colorful species such as cardinals, blue jays, robins and more. Rural woodlands and fields offer year-round habitats for many species threatened by urban encroachment and resting places for migrating species.

Yet children grow to maturity without noting the difference between the grackle's grating call and the sweet song of the robin. The hoot of the owl is just a noise on a Tootsie Pop commercial.

Attracting birds to your garden offers a simple solution. For under $10, you can start with a simple feeder hung near a window so that the smallest child in your home can view the birds. Children naturally love birds. They bring something of the wild right to our doorsteps. Their colors and antics delight young and old alike.

As children mature, identifying birds using a good guidebook such as the *Peterson's Field Guide* helps cultivate attention to detail among children. As you'll learn in this book, noticing the smallest details helps you identify each bird species. Such exercises develop awareness, attention to detail, deductive thinking and reasoning skills in small children. And just maybe the adults in your household need a little help, too!

Helping Endangered and Threatened Species

Attracting, feeding and caring for wild birds also supports threatened and endangered species. As the urban and suburban sprawl continues throughout the United States, many woodland and meadow habitats once used by migrating and nesting birds have disappeared. Birds adapt as much as they can, but providing some special nesting boxes, food and other items they need provides much-valued support for birds in danger from human activities. Hanging a bluebird house on a fence post may not seem like much, but to the lovely and threatened bluebird, it provides a safe space to raise a clutch of young. One house can help bluebirds raise 3 to 6 chicks per year; think of how many birds you will help with just one house!

Enjoying the Colorful Show

So what is the best reason to attract birds to the garden? For me, it's the sheer pleasure of watching them throughout the year. I love noticing the wildlife in my garden from the smallest toad to the large vultures perusing the woods for carrion. My parents fed the birds in our tiny urban/suburban yard and my favorite memories are of my father holding out his hand with a bit of bird seed on it while chickadee plucked seeds right from his hands. My mother taught me the names of birds in our suburban neighborhood while pushing my stroller down the block as she ran errands. I learned to distinguish cardinals from blue jays, sparrows from crows; simple birds for a child to identify and common birds in an urban and suburban environment.

Watching birds is fun. On a snowy winter morning, it's wonderful to peer out the kitchen window at the bird feeder and watch brilliant cardinals on the feeder. I love seeing migrating birds on our farm and have spied many that I never thought I would see.

As with all gardening activities, attracting birds to the garden can be as complicated or as simple as you like. This book is intended to be a beginner's guide to attracting birds. There are many advanced books on the market, but as I talk to people interested in bird watching and feeding, they feel intimidated by the language, the complicated scientific information and all the so-called 'rules' about feeding birds.

Start with a simple bird feeder and add on as your budget, time and interest allows. Fortunately, attracting birds to your garden is easy if you have patience. Give birds what they naturally need and just wait; sooner or later, they will flock to your garden.

Chapter One: What Attracts Birds to the Garden?

Birds are wild creatures. We tame them or keep them as pets, but at heart they remain wild, more at home in nature than in a cage in the house. The secret to attracting a wide variety of wild birds to the garden is to provide them with the ideal aspects of their natural habitat. Entice birds into your garden or yard by using their natural instincts to your advantage.

Think of it this way. What attracts you to a living space? Let's say you're apartment hunting. The real estate agent hands you a list of properties within your price rang and within the same zip code. Off you go to inspect them. Some of the apartments don't have elevators and you think about the hot summer days ahead when you'll have to trudge up six flights of stairs carrying grocery bags. Other apartments have tiny kitchens. One doesn't have a bathtub, just a small shower unit in the corner.

Finally you find the perfect apartment. It's got a large living room, two bedrooms, a great kitchen and a new bathroom. Best of all, it's on the third floor of a building that has an elevator. It's within several blocks of the grocery store so you can walk to the store to do your shopping.

It's also near your workplace, so you won't have a long commute. It's the perfect place for your family.

Birds consider similar aspects when choosing which yards to visit. What attracts wild birds to the yard?

Food: Each species of bird eats a different diet. Some prefer seeds while others eat only insects. Some peck food from the ground while others hang parallel to tree trunks and use their sharp, pointy beak to peck out insects from the bark. As you begin your bird feeding adventures, a simple seed feeder filled with a songbird or similar mix attracts a variety of birds to the garden. Later on you can add other types of feeders and food to attract different species.

Water: Birds need water year-round, and during the winter months a water supply becomes even more critical. Natural water features such as ponds and creeks are ideal, but simple bird baths work well too in the home garden.

Shelter: Shelter ensures that birds have a safe spot to hide from predators and perch at night. Create a natural habitat for birds by planting trees and shrubs that provide shelter for birds. You don't need to buy rare or exotic plants; native species are actually better for attracting birds, and you probably already have many shrubs and trees they like in your yard already.

Nesting sites: During the spring and summer months, birds seek nesting sites to hatch and raise their young. Bird houses attract mating pairs to the yard and it's fun to watch them raise their young. You may be surprised, however, at how adaptable birds are; they find nesting sites in the oddest places. One year we had a nest of Phoebes, an insect-eating bird, on the ceiling fan on our front porch. My husband duct-taped the fan blades to the porch roof to ensure that the wind wouldn't spin the babies right off the fan! It was great fun for us (and our cat) to sit in the living room and watch the birds hatch, grow and finally fledge or fly away. While not essential to begin a bird feeding and watching hobby, nesting sites add an extra dimension to your new hobby and attract birds to the garden.

Building on Birds' Natural Instincts

Obviously, birds find all four items on their shopping list in the wild. Like all wild creatures, birds inherit an instinctual knowledge of how to find what they need, and may also learn some skills from observing their parents. To attract birds to your garden, you have to understand the instincts of wild birds, especially birds native to your area, and create a site that they find attractive.

According to some sources, 796 species of birds live in North America. About 8,650 species of birds have been identified worldwide. The types of birds you can attract to your garden depend on where you live and the natural landscape around you. Think about it: penguins may love the Antarctic, but they're unlikely to waddle their way into a city park outside a New York City brownstone (unless they escape from a zoo). A New York City bird lover can enjoy sparrows, pigeons, cardinals, blue jays, and hawks from her balcony window, and many more species, but she's unlikely to see an Indigo bunting or bluebird. Conversely, where I live in rural Virginia, I never see pigeons, but we have many bluebirds including some nesting in boxes provided near our vegetable garden. The types of birds who visit your garden depend on where you live.

Each species of bird has adapted to its unique habitat and climate. Birds eat a wide variety of food, including spiders, worms, grubs, insects, nectar from flowers, berries and small fruits, nuts, tree sap, eggs and baby birds stolen from other nests (it's sad but true), snails, and even road kill.

Chances are you're not interested in attracting vultures to the garden by laying out road kill, so let's focus on common types of birds to attract to the garden and the natural elements they seek. By replicating the natural environment as much as you can, you can attract each type to the garden.

Seed Eaters

Have you ever noticed that each bird's bill is shaped differently? Seed eaters have short, cone-shaped bills perfect for cutting open small seed capsules and cracking seeds open. Many have brightly colored plumage too, making them particularly attractive to watch.

Common seed eating birds you can attract to the garden include:

Cardinals

Finches

Grosbeaks

American sparrows

Junco

Pine Siskin

Of course there are many, many more seed eating birds, and the exact species that may visit your garden depends on where you live.

Seed eating birds need seeds year-round but may supplement their diet with insects. Don't get confused if you see sparrow hop up with an insect in its mouth. Many species supplement their diet with insects during spring when raising their young. The additional protein from the insects helps their babies develop and grow.

Woodpeckers and Other Insect-Seeking Birds

Woodpeckers seek insects by using their bills to feel for vibrations in trees, logs, branches and other natural objects caused by insects. Their sharp, chiseled bills then peck holes into the trees until they find the insects hidden deep within. Sometimes they get confused by vibrations in other materials. In the suburban/urban town where I grew up, we had a woodpecker who visited my neighbor's aerial television antenna each night, pecking away at the metal. The wind made the metal antenna vibrate, fooling the woodpecker into thinking he had a meal waiting! The poor bird kept this up for a long, long time.

Other species of birds seek insects by climbing along the trunk of trees and pecking, so find and use a good bird guide to learn the various species that inhabit your area.

Swallows, robins and many other kinds of birds also eat insects. Swallow fly low over fields, meadows and even roadways, snatching flying insects from the sky. They have wide bills with tiny bristles on them that make the perfect "net" for catching insects in mid-flight. Robins and others peck at the ground to find worms, larvae, and hidden insects. Their bills aren't suitable for cracking open seeds, so during times when insects are scarce they may seek and eat soft fruits like berries.

Birds that Eat Meat

Finally, some birds eat flesh or carrion. Flesh-eating birds include owls, who swoop down and capture small rodents and other creatures to dine on. These nocturnal birds are difficult to see in the wild; you're much more likely to hear their cries, ranging from the typical "whoo-whoo-WHOO" to the blood-curdling shriek of the screech owl. A great website is the Ornithology Laboratory at Cornell University, which has recordings of all the major species of owls found in North America. If you think you've heard an owl late at night, listen to the various recordings to identify your owl. And lest you think owls only inhabit unpopulated areas, my brother, who lives in a Long Island suburban housing development, discovered a nest of screech owls in an oak tree across the street from his house when a baby screech owl tumbled out of the nest! They brought the owl to a local bird sanctuary who finished raising it and released it back into the wild. Even in the midst of the most built up, populated areas, wildlife finds a way to adapt.

Hawks, falcons and kestrels are birds of prey that eat small animals. Vultures eat carrion and flesh foods too, soaring high above the ground to seek their foods. Some birds such as crows have bills adapted to eat almost anything, and you will find these birds in almost any type of environment.

Nectar Feeding Birds

Among the birds I've mentioned, none have fascinated me as much as hummingbirds. With their curving needle-like beaks, these tiny birds seek nectar-producing flowers and sip the nectar for energy. Feeding hummingbirds is a unique task in and unto itself, and these tiny birds have a curious, friendly nature that draws them very close to the home when you feed them.

As you can see from the brief descriptions above, each species of bird has evolved to fill a unique niche in the environment. Birds flock to the garden when their natural food sources are abundant. Birds can eat their weight in insects in one evening, helping to reduce mosquito populations. They nibble at seeds and sometimes get pesky stealing raspberries or strawberries from the backyard garden. But it's finding a natural source of food that ultimately attracts them to the garden.

Natural Water Sources

Before humans put up housing developments and paved over everything, nature provided water for birds through creeks, springs, ponds, lakes, rivers and streams. Mankind diverted, paved over, and polluted many of these natural sources. Urban sprawl hides the rest under miles of concrete. Birds still find water, but drink from standing puddles in roadways or oil-soaked water in parking lots.

While it's not necessary to add a water source to your backyard bird garden, a simple birdbath is inexpensive and adds a clean water source as long as you rinse or scrub it when algae begins to grow. In urban and suburban areas, such a birdbath may provide a welcome source of clean water, particularly during hot days when natural puddles or rainwater is absent.

Colorful, Beautiful Birds

Why do some birds have brightly colored plumage and others sport shades of gray, rust and brown? Think about the natural habitat of each bird species.

Birds live in certain areas of the natural world, feeding, mating, and drinking among specific terrains. Each terrain has different natural coloring. Birds that survive in that terrain usually have feathers that mimic the environment so that predators are less likely to see them.

One afternoon last winter, I was walking my dog down our driveway. The driveway to our farm is about a quarter of a mile long and once it crests the top of a hill, it winds its way through a bit of woodland before coming to the road and two houses. As I walked my dog through the woodland bit, I saw a blur of motion to our right. I had to stop and really stare into the woods before I could make out the brown and white puffy features of quail. A flock of quail were feeding along the grassy strip between the gravel driveway and the woods, and our approach scattered them deep into the cover of the forest. The fallen leaves, branches and twigs provided hiding places for these shy birds and their brown feathers blended perfectly into the natural environment. If they held still I would never have seen them.

Some birds have bright plumage. Bright blue or green feathers, for example, may seem counter-intuitive given the needs for feathers to hide the bird, but among sun-dappled summer tree leaves, blue and green actually become camouflage.

As for the cardinal's bright red and the blue jay's blue, I don't know what nature was thinking. But I'm sure grateful for the variety and diversity of birds!

Should You Focus on Specific Species?

Given this very brief discussion of how birds differ and fill selected ecological niches, you may wonder if you should focus your bird feeding efforts on specific species or just put food out and hope for the best.

Start simple. If you jump in feet first and buy all sorts of feeders and feed, you may lose interest or find that other tasks take time away from your enjoyment of feeding the birds. Conversely, if you start small and hang one feeder with an inexpensive seed mixture, your delight and joy from watching the birds visit each morning may grow into a life-long hobby. You can always add more items to your bird feeding area later on. I recommend starting with a simple mixture that attracts the largest variety of birds to your area, and you can specialize and individualize later.

Chapter Two: Feeding Wild Birds

I hope that this brief introduction to the life of birds in the wild has been helpful to you. Learning these facts helped me understand and appreciate what birds needed in the garden to feel secure and comfortable, and what elements attracted the most birds over time. Now let's move on to the specifics of feeding wild birds in the backyard garden.

Seed Feeders

The most common type of bird feeder is the seed feeder, and this is where you should begin your bird feeding adventures if you've never fed the birds before. Seed feeders come in a wide range of sizes, styles and types, ranging from the purely practical to the whimsical.

The concept of seed feeders is simple. Provide a place to hold the seed, a perch for the birds to sit and eat, and a feeding area conducive to the bird's natural instinct to feed.

Some common seed feeders available at garden centers and stores include:

Hanging Feeders: Hanging feeders come in many sizes, shapes and materials. Many look like little bird houses with a roof, a center "house" portion to hold the seed, and a tray underneath. Gravity pulls the seeds down through the center portion as the birds eat. You can use an economical seed mixture containing millet, thistle, nyjer and sunflowers in any type of hanging feeder with good success. Stay clear of the types that hang outside the windows using suction cups. The suction cups never hold them for long on the windowsill as the weight of the seed and the birds landing on the feeders pulls them right off the window. You'll spend more time hanging your feeder than you will enjoying the birds.

Tube Feeders: Tube feeders are made from a clear, heavy duty plastic. They can be of any size but consist of a long cylinder or tube of plastic with holes in the sides rimmed with metal and metal perches. A metal bottom with a cork-shaped cleaning port and a metal cap that slides off the top complete the feeder. These feeders are ideal for more expensive brands of seeds and for feeding specific types of birds. Finches, Pine Siskins and other small birds flock to tube feeders filled with thistle and sunflower seeds. Invest in a good quality tube feeder such as one made by the Droll Yankee company. Higher quality tube feeders use special metal alloys that do not freeze and are easier on the birds' feed in winter months. They're also easier to clean. I prefer tube feeders and have two, one large and one small. I fill the large one with an economical seed mixture and the smaller one with sunflower seeds. Any seeds knocked out of the feeder to the ground attract ground feeders such as mourning doves, providing me with a nice variety of birds.

Suet Feeders: Birds need some protein and fat, especially in the winter months. Suet provides both. Commercial suet blends made from beef or mutton fat are sold in blocks or cakes. A suet feeder is a simple metal cage that holds the commercial block of suet. Many suet blocks also contains nuts, seeds and berries, and each appeals to different kinds of birds. They're inexpensive and last for several weeks unless an enterprising squirrel gets a hold of it. I've also seen woodpeckers and flickers help themselves to suet, a nice treat in the middle of winter. Suet feeders are inexpensive, and the metal cages last a long time. The blocks of suet fat hold their shape under about 70 degrees but begin to melt as temperatures rise, so wait to hang a suet feeder until the weather is consistently cold. You can also make a simple suet feeder from pine cones, bacon fat or peanut butter and bird seed. I'll share the recipe and instructions in Chapter Six.

Tray Feeders: Some species of birds eat from the ground. They peck at the seeds near the ground and do not like hanging feeders, although you may find them on a hanging feeder, especially those with larger trays. A tray feeder is a small tray or box-shaped feeder that is placed on the ground with some seeds in it. You don't need to buy anything fancy. I use a clean pie plate left over from a frozen apple pie or some such and put a big rock in the center to weigh it down. Then I add the seed. That's it. You can scatter seeds on the ground too for the same effect as long as you place the seeds in an area where weeds won't matter. Some birdseed brands do take root and grow grassy-type weeds. Squirrels and other creatures such as mice and rats may also be attracted to tray feeders placed on the ground, so if you go this route do place them far away from buildings and homes. You don't want to attract all the local wildlife to your home!

Hummingbird Feeders: I've saved what I think is perhaps the most fun bird feeder for last, the hummingbird feeder. Hummingbirds are fascinating little creatures. They're tiny birds with whirring wings that drink nectar from flowers. Hummingbird feeders provide liquid, sugar infused nectar for the little birds. Each feeder consists of a bottle of some sort with ports shaped like flowers to entice the hummingbirds over for a nip. Hummingbirds are warm-weather birds and migrate to warmer climates, so place your feeders outside from around April to October (or thereabouts, depending on where you live...northern gardeners can put the feeders out a bit later, while southern gardeners should provide hummingbirds with nectar for a tad bit longer.) Plastic and glass hummingbird feeders are available and while both provide satisfactory feeding stations, I've found glass ones a little easier to keep clean. Cleanliness is the most important aspect of feeding hummingbirds, since the sugar-infused nectar tends to generate mold on the feeder and attract various insects, which have a tendency to get into the feeder and drown. Hang your hummingbird feeder near a porch, deck or window to enjoy the antics of these tiny jewel-like birds. Hummingbirds are naturally curious, sociable birds, and many will come as close as they dare to check out the strange "birds" watching them!

Seeds and Feeds

During the winter months, you can pick up a package of bird seed at any grocery store, hardware store, feed store, or nursery and garden center. But what's in each bag of seed?

Most seed mixtures contain the following in varying amounts:

Millet – tiny beadlike seeds from the grain, millet

Thistle or **Nyjer** – also spelled niger (NYE-jer) these are small nutritious seeds

Sunflower seeds – either whole sunflowers or the center portion, but most likely whole sunflowers

Corn – some seed mixtures contain dried corn kernels

Fillers – the least expensive brands of sunflower seeds may contain more filler types of grass seeds

A good quality mixture contains higher proportions of sunflower seeds, nyjer and thistle. You can also purchase bags of only one type of seed, such as bags of black oil sunflower seeds (the most nutrient dense and rich of all sunflower seeds) or nyjer. By placing only one type of seed in a feeder, you'll attract a specific type of bird. To get started attracting, feeding and watching birds, I recommend a simple mix.

Mixing Your Own Birdseed

Some backyard bird aficionados like to mix their own bird seed recipe. If you'd like to try your own mixture, here is the basic recipe. Be sure to have a bucket or pail with a tight fitting cover to hold unused mix.

Basic Backyard Birdseed Mix Recipe

Sunflower seeds, hulled, oil type	50-60%
Millet seeds	30%
Cracked corn, fine	10-20%

When to Begin Feeding the Birds

You can start feeding birds at any time during the year. Feeding the birds year round won't make them dependent on birdseed. Fewer birds visit the feeder in the summer; they'll find natural food sources whenever possible, supplementing what nature provides by visits to the backyard feeder.

I take my bird feeders down in the early spring for a variety of reasons. First of all, by the time spring rolls around the local squirrel population has found the feeders, and I find they eat their way through an entire tube feeder's worth of seeds in one afternoon faster than I can replace it. I end up feeding squirrels more than birds, and considering that I live on a tree farm with a large stand of hickory nut trees near the road, it's obvious to me that I'm feeding gourmet fare to the gray beasts rather than supporting them through tough winter months; they have plenty of nuts stashed around my farm, trust me. I also like to take down the feeders and give them a good cleaning.

I begin feeding the hummingbirds in early April. Typically, I wait until I see the first hummingbirds appear in my area of Virginia before I fill their feeder. I use a commercial powder mixed with water, but sugar water can also be used to fill their feeders. I keep the feeders up until the end of October. Hummingbirds migrate through our area until mid October, but I've seen a straggler or two as late as Halloween, and fewer wildflowers bloom in my area at that time of year, wildflowers that produce natural nectar sources. I hope that I am supplementing their feed as much as a I can.

I'll fill the first bird feeders here on the farm in early November when the evenings dip into the thirties and forties. I move my feeders around from year to year, never hanging them in the same space twice, both to thwart the squirrels and to enjoy a different view. I prefer to hang feeders on tree such as dogwoods, where the branching structure of the tree provides multiple perching sites and berries provide supplemental food.

I use a simple chain purchased from the hardware store and spring-hook to hang my tube feeders. I loop a length of chain over a pine tree branch and slip it through the metal loop at the top of the tube feeder, closing the chain with the spring hook. I've also hung a length of heavy-duty chain between two trees and suspended each tube feeder from the chain using spring hooks. While this method kept the squirrels at bay longer than the other, it was more difficult for me to reach the feeders and fill them, especially when snow covered the garden and I could not get a ladder out to the pines to fill them.

Some tray feeders and hanging-feeder types can be fixed to the top of a heavy steel pole. My dad used to use this method, placing a thick steel pole into the same hole and cup that my mom used in the summer months for our laundry-drying tree. He'd use chocks of wood to steady it. Later on, he simply dug a deeper hole and used dirt to hold it in place after we stopped using the laundry pole. Vaseline rubbed onto the pole during the winter months kept all but the most tenacious squirrel from ascending the pole to nibble seeds above.

Hang suet feeders on tree branches or against the trunks of trees. I've found that those placed against the trunks of trees attract woodpeckers and flickers the best.

Remember to keep tray feeders for ground-feeding birds away from houses, buildings and structures as these can attract vermin. If using a pie plate or an old baking tray as a ground feeding station, place bricks or rocks on the edges to keep the wind and animals from tripping it over.

Storing Bird Seed

Store birdseed in the garage or an outdoor shed. I learned the hard way to place the plastic bags of birdseed inside big buckets with tight-fitting lids. One year I simply lined up the plastic bags of seed along the garage wall. I didn't think twice about it. As I worked my way through the first bags, I noticed a trail of seed leading away from the line of bags, but I thought I'd just spilled some seed as I carried my scoop and coffee can full of seed out to the feeders. A few weeks later my husband brought his car to the mechanic for its annual state inspection. The mechanic called to tell us he found mice nesting in the engine compartment! Luckily for us, they'd built their nest away from the mechanical parts or we could have had serious problems. As we investigated, we realized that a colony of intrepid field mice had set up housekeeping near the birdseed. I had a roll of old carpet in the back of the garage, which we'd spread on the ground while changing the oil in the cars or doing outdoor work. The mice had built nests inside the carpet roll and in the car engine. They gnawed holes in the plastic bags and were feasting on the birdseed, leaving a trail of seed behind. Removing their nests and catching the mice took some time, but the few we caught were released far away in the woods. Seed is now kept in tight plastic drums that so far have withstood any potential rodent attacks. I learned the hard way to keep seed away from hungry critters. I can only imagine how those mice must have felt upon finding a nice soft roll of carpet and a ready supply of food; they must have thought they landed in mouse heaven!

Easy Bird Feeding

Do yourself a big favor. Hang your bird feeders in spaces that are easy for you to access on a regular basis. Keep in mind that birds need to eat regardless of the weather, so be sure that your feeder is assessable during snowstorms, too. I made that mistake once by hanging my feeders on tall trees that required a ladder to reach and fill. After receiving a foot of snow one cold January day, I couldn't access the now-empty feeders. How frustrating it was to sit inside the house watching empty feeders swing in the wind! And if I was frustrated, what did the birds think?

I keep an empty coffee can and a garden trowel in the garage to carry seed from the pails to the feeders. I fill the coffee can and then use the trowel to scoop seed from the can into the tube feeders. Other hanging feeders with wide apertures are easier to fill; simply pour the seed into the top.

Shopping List: What You Need

Take this list to the store and get started feeding the birds.

Feeder – seed feeder, either hanging type ($10-$15) or tube feeder ($20 and up)
Seed – bag of bird seed mix ($5 - $10 for a 20 pound bag) or single bags of selected seeds (prices vary)
Chain and **spring hook**

Bird Feeding Frequently Asked Questions

If I feed the birds, do they get dependent on my feeder? If I stop will they die?

No! This is by far the most frequently asked question about backyard bird feeding. Wild birds are adaptable and enjoy food you put out for them. Birds who visit your garden also forage among the shrubs, trees and plants in the area for additional food. They never lose their ability to find food in the wild even if they enjoy eating at your bird feeder year 'round. So go ahead and feed the birds!

If I pick the wrong seed, will I hurt any birds?

Birds select and eat the feed they need and like. If it's not the right kind of food for them, they won't eat it.

Is there a surefire way to keep squirrels off my bird feeder?

Unfortunately, no. Squirrels are smart and adaptable and the only way to keep them off is to actually remove the feeder. You can try the many tricks outlined in this book, but sometimes the squirrels will outwit you!

Can I use leftover garden seeds in the feeder?

Not a good idea. Some seeds are coated or made into pellets and the coating may make birds sick. Stick to birdseed sold in bags and marked as birdseed.

Chapter Three: Plants that Attract Birds

A feeder is a great first step to attract birds to the backyard garden. Once the birds find your garden and eat from your feeder, they'll return year after year if you provide them with a garden filled with plants and accessories that meet their needs for food, water, shelter, and nesting sites. You can add one shrub that appeals to birds or plant your entire garden as a bird sanctuary. The choices is yours; keep it as simple or as complex as you like.

Importance of Organic Gardening Practice

Before considering the tree, shrubs and other plants to add to the garden to attract birds, I'd like to bring up the subject of organic gardening practices. Organic gardening is a holistic method of gardening that builds the soil and the garden ecosystem while eschewing the use of chemical fertilizers and pesticides. It's a complicated subject, with whole books written about it, and it is outside the scope of this beginner's guide to attracting birds to the garden. It is, however, an important topic if you want to nurture the wildlife in your part of the world.

In the opening chapters, I wrote at length about the natural diet of wild birds. As you may recall, birds eat a variety of food, including insects. Most birds eat some type of insect for protein during the nesting and fledging portion of their life cycle. This extra protein builds strong eggshells. Shells that crack or are too weak to support the embryonic birds cannot sustain life and the baby birds die. Similarly, protein from insects builds strong baby birds, helping them grow and develop properly.

Consider the cycle of nature. Insects feed upon plants. Birds feed upon insects. They pass along the insects, regurgitating them in palatable form to their young.

Chemical fertilizers added to the garden dissolve into the soil. The plant's roots absorb the fertilizers through moisture in the soil. The vascular system transports water and chemicals throughout the entire plant. As insects nibble on plants, they ingest whatever the plant ingested. They in turn pass this along to the birds that eat them. Chemical pesticides sprayed onto leaves readily transfer to the insects. Birds swooping down into the garden snatching insects from leaves may snatch up an insect that has just ingested a lethal dose of malathion or another chemical constituent that could harm the bird. That's a meal the birds didn't bargain for, and a meal they should do without.

While adhering to organic gardening practices sounds time-consuming and difficult, it's actually fairly easy – as long as you don't mind the occasional nibbled leaf or imperfect tomato. The truth is that most of us are so used to the glossy, perfect produce at the supermarket that we've forgotten that nature is imperfect. Tomatoes have spots and dots, carrots can be lumpy and misshapen, and flowers don't always look perfect. Would you rather have a healthy garden ecosystem or perfect tomatoes? There's no one right answer. But choosing to use organic gardening methods does indeed boost the health of the overall ecosystem, including the birds visiting your bird feeding station.

Attracting Birds: Creating a Natural Habitat

Planting a bird garden enhances the natural landscape and provides plant sources of food, shelter, nesting materials and more for birds. It takes its cues from the landscape surrounding the garden, enhancing and building upon what nature provides.

For people like me who live in a rural environment, it's easy to see what nature provides. A glance outside my window reveals elderberry and sumac dripping with ripe fruit, a favorite snack for many birds. Each summer my Echinacea patch in the flower garden receives dozens of bright American goldfinches who love to eat the newly formed seed heads; the same goes for my stand of sunflowers, where birds devour seeds faster than I can store them for the winter.

Yet even in urban or suburban environments clues exist as to what the original terrain looked like. Vacant lots and any tract of land that still stands empty of housing and concrete yields telltale signs. Central Park, although a designed and manicured park, attracts certain wild birds; local parks, lots, and yards often echo the original landscape of the area. A good reference guide or your local County Cooperative Extension may also help.

Ask for materials that help you select "native plants." These are trees, shrubs, annuals and perennials that may be found in the wild in your area. Such plants are not only sought-after by the bird, they are also less prone to disease and better able to withstand the weather conditions unique to your area. Nature adapted them over the centuries to the weather, terrain, and other conditions in the area, and as such they're less fussy and easier to care for than many other plants.

Landscapes Birds Love

Luckily for the average backyard gardener, the habitat humans provide by planting lawns, gardens and foundation plantings creates a landscape most birds enjoy. Walls and fences provide perching places; foundation plants provide shelter, and garden plants provide food, nesting sites and shelter. You don't need a huge garden to attract birds either; a small backyard is just fine.

Bird gardens do not follow any one particular style. They may be informal, with simple flowers beds and trees, or formal and meticulously clipped. While birds tend to prefer rough, ragged hedges and naturally shaped plants, they'll still come for a visit if you love your topiary or your clipped box hedge.

The key to planting a landscape that birds love is variety. The ideal bird garden contains some mature, tall trees and some shorter trees. The tall trees provide nesting and resting sites for birds and, depending upon the tree, perhaps nuts and seeds, too.

But here's the best part about planting a garden to attract birds; birds don't care whether it's your garden or your next door neighbor's garden. They fly where they will without regard to boundaries, fences, or property lines. If you live near a water reclamation area or sump, they'll enjoy it as if it were a lake, and use it as their water source. If you have a park within a few miles, they'll take advantage of the mature trees in the park for nesting sites and visit your feeder for seed.

Adding trees, shrubs, grasses and flowering plants to the garden provides addition resources for the birds and excuses for them to linger longer.

Plants that Attract Birds

The following list of plants that attract birds will vary depending on where you live. People living in the western section of the United States or in desert areas will need to find a list of plants suitable for their conditions. Your local County Cooperative Extension Office provides a treasure-trove of free pamphlets, flyers and advice. They're sure to have a list of suitable plants to add to the landscape to support birds in your area.

The majority of gardeners in the United States from zones 5 through 8 can plant any of the following to attract birds to the garden.

Choosing Plants

You do not need to add all of the plants below. If you have a mature landscape and a garden already, just add a few of the plants on the list as time and space allows. Any plants that you add will increase the chances that birds will visit your garden, and will enhance your bird watching experience.

Small Plants to Attract Birds: Annuals

Annual plants are plants that grow, flower, and die with the frost. They may reseed in a particular area but the original plant does not return from year to year. Many species of birds love these annuals for their flowers and seeds. Some, like Bachelor's Buttons (Centauria cyanus) are easily grown from seed in a sunny location. Others may be purchased as plants at the garden center in the spring

Amaratnhus

Bachelor Button (Centauria cyanus)

Calendula (Calendula officianalis)

Coreopsis

Cosmos

Gloriosa daisy

Love in a Mist (Nigella damascene)

Marigolds

Pinks (Dianthus)

Portulaca

Sunflowers

Zinnias

Perennials to Attract Birds

Perennials are plants that return year after year from roots or rhizomes. They may die back entirely to the ground and push forth new growth in the spring or return from woody portions remaining above the ground. Many of these perennials provide attractive foliage, such as grasses, or lovely flowers—but it's the seeds the birds are after. Watch your perennials after they've flowered and gone to seed and observe which birds choose to visit. If you can beat the birds to the seeds, save seeds and grow more to add to the garden next year.

Aster

Black Eyed Susan (Rudbeckia)

Butterfly Flower (Asclepias tuberosa)

Chrysanthemums

Columbine

Coreopsis, perennial types

Echinacea – all species

Perennial grasses of all types

Small Trees Attractive to Wild Birds

If you have room to add a tree to your garden, the following small trees attract many types of birds. They also add areas from which to hang bird feeders.

Crab apple

Dogwood, many types including Corenlia cherry, Kousa and flowering dogwood

Japanese maple

Hawthorn

Hemlocks

Holly

Maple (smaller types)

Serviceberry (Amelanchier)

Shrubs and Trees that Produce Fruit

Many colorful birds love the fruit provided by these trees. Before planting these trees, consider their location and whether or not the fruits falling to the ground will bother you or create an unsightly area in the garden. Some, such as the Elderberry and Mulberry, can make quite the mess, and birds perching for hours on the branches and nibbling at the fruits poop all over the surrounding area. If it's out in the woods or in a corner of the garden it may not be a problem, but if the only area suitable for such a tree is near your sidewalk, pool or patio, you may want to forego a fruiting tree. If you do choose to plant a tree that produces fruit, the following attract the widest variety of birds.

Bayberry

Blackberry

Blueberry

Wild cherry

Currents

Elderberry

Firethorn

Hawthorn

Holly

Honeysuckle

Mountain Ash

Roses (yes, they're shrubs)

Serviceberry

Spicebush

Sumac

Vibrnum (many types but not all)

Other Trees

Other trees that you may wish to add for nesting sites and hiding places for birds include the following list. They're fast-growing, which adds to their appeal for suburban homeowners looking for quick gardens or screening trees. Remember to check the height and the root habit and look at the site where you want to add the tree. You don't want a tall tree blocking all the sunlight from your flower and vegetable garden, nor do you want deep roots cracking your septic and water lines. When in doubt, talk to someone at your local garden center or Cooperative Extension office.

Alder

Birch

Hackberry

Pine (Eastern White Pine)

Oaks (Pin Oak and Red Oak)

Poplar

Red Maple

Sweet Gum

Tulip Tree

Shrubs for Hedges

Birds love to perch in hedges. While they prefer hedges left on the wild side, even a manicured hedge provides refuge for them and nesting places. The following shrubs make good bird-friendly hedges.

Boxwood

Cherry laurel

Firethorn

Holly – Chinese holly, Japanese holly

Japanese barberry

Juniper

Myrtle

Privet

Yew

Plants for Hummingbirds

Hummingbirds need specific plants. Their long, needle-like beaks sip nectar, and they seek sweet flowers with tube or trumpet-like shapes. Many plants that attract and feed hummingbirds are also excellent for butterfly gardens too, providing a delightful shower of color as both hummingbirds and butterflies visit such plants during the height of summer.

Hummingbird are attracted to red, pink and orange flowers. Plant flowers in clusters so that the burst of color catches their attention. Choose the following annuals (A) and perennials (P) to entice hummingbirds into the garden.

Achillea (P)

Geranium (A)

Gladiolus (A/P)

Hibiscus (P)

Hosta (P)

Morning Glory (A)

Penstemmon (P)

Scabiosa (P)

Sedum (P)

Zinnia (A)

Enjoy Your Garden

One of the great joys of attracting birds to the garden is that many of the plants that people enjoy for their beautiful form, color or fragrance are also enjoyed by birds. Plant your garden for your own personal enjoyment. Birds aren't fussy about style. Give them the basics, and they will visit your garden, stopping by with a cheery hello to feed, drink and play.

Chapter Four: Providing Water and Shelter

All living creatures need food, water and shelter, and birds are no exception. We've discussed food sources including plants that provide natural food sources. Now let's talk about the two other items birds need: water and shelter.

Water Sources for Birds

Nature provides many opportunities for birds to drink and bathe, from streams and creeks to puddles after rainstorms. Most landscapes actually contain enough water sources for birds. Even the concrete jungles of the inner city offer pools of water after rainstorms or small enclaves such as parks with a pond or two.

Rural and suburban gardeners needn't worry either. Remember that birds fly over property boundaries; they'll visit your neighbor's pond or the local creeks for water as needed.

So why bother providing a water source if birds fend for themselves? Bird baths provide lovely focal points and accents in the garden. It's fun to watch birds splash and play in the water, and it provides yet one more attractive feature to make the birds choose your yard or garden over another one to visit.

Birdbaths

Birdbaths come in many sizes, styles, materials and colors. The most common types include concrete, resin and plastic.

Concrete birdbaths are heavy. They are made by pouring concrete into molds and are often sold in two parts, the saucer or dish top and the pedestal base. The dish should be wide and shallow to facilitate bathing.

Resin birdbaths may be heavy or lightweight, depending on the style and quality. Some resin birdbaths have a plug in the bottom of the pedestal. You're supposed to fill the pedestal with sand, then plug the hole to weigh down the birdbath so that the wind won't blow it over. I have a small resin birdbath and find that the birds don't use it. I like its decorative appeal, so I keep it in the rose garden. I've tried plastic birdbaths and personally do not feel that they are worth the money. They tip over too easy and it's annoying to constantly run outside and fix them.

No matter which style you choose, be sure to do the following to make your birdbath attractive to wild birds:

Make sure it's level. A level birdbath is less likely to tip over. If the ground is uneven, use dirt or sand to create a level section. I have a backyard with a considerable slope and used dirt to level a section, then placed a slate over it to make a firm foundation.

Fill the center pedestal with sand if you buy a plastic birdbath. This will make it heavier and less likely to tip.

Place the birdbath under a tree such as a dogwood if you have one. Not only does it make a pretty focal point, birds have a place close by to perch and wait their turn.

Keep it filled. If it constantly runs dry, birds won't return. Birds crave reliable water sources and a constantly filled birdbath helps.

Scrub it down regularly. Algae and molds not only detract from the birdbaths appearance, they can make birds sick. I bought a scrub brush at the local dollar store. It hangs in the garage near where I store my birdseed, to that I can grab both seed and brush for quick trips out to the garden. I just spray the birdbath with water to loosen the algae, scrub, rinse and refill. It takes only about five minutes to clean a birdbath and I tackle it about once a week (sometimes more frequently in the summer).

Storing the Birdbath

Unless you use a birdbath heater (see below) you must drain and store the birdbath before freezing weather arrives. Water freezing and thawing in a concrete birdbath can crack the basin. You can leave the heavy pedestal outside, but empty the birdbath basin and store it in a garage, shed or basement until the spring. Replace, refill and enjoy after all danger of frost is past.

Resin and plastic birdbaths may be able to withstand the winter temperatures, but I've found they last longer if you store them in the same manner as concrete birdbaths. So dump out the water and carry them inside; it will make them last longer.

Winter Water Supply

Water tends to be in short supply for birds during peak winter months as ponds, creeks and puddles freeze. That's when using a device called a birdbath heater comes in handy. Such heaters keep the water from freezing. They're not essential, but if you can afford one and are interested in using one, visit your local nursery or garden center or specialty store like Wild Birds Unlimited. Follow the directions for use.

Birdhouses: Shelter and Nesting Sites

Birdhouses offer birds places for nesting. In the wild, birds select a wide range of nesting sites ranging from cliffs to shrubs. They build a variety of nests – cup shaped, ground nests, twigs and leaves, grasses and more. As people have encroached on their natural habits, birds have adapted. Swallows nest in the eaves of barns or porches. Pigeons, crows and sparrows use neon signs to build nests. The local Home Depot had to put guards on their big "HOME DEPOT" sign because the letter O seemed to be an attractive spot for the local pigeon population to build their nests, creating quite the mess each spring! When I worked at a major garden center, sparrows built nests inside the hanging baskets in the Annuals area; the poor manager of the area was constantly hiding the baskets in the back so the boss wouldn't make her destroy the nests so he could sell the baskets. Here on our rural property, a nesting pair of Phoebes decided that the ceiling fan on our front porch made an ideal nesting site. Within a day the nest was built, but winds turning the fan blades threatened to topple nest, eggs and all onto the porch. My intrepid spouse duct-taped the fan blades to the ceiling until the babies fledged and we could take down the fan and clean off the nest.

Given birds' amazing ability to adapt to their environment, why provide nesting boxes or birdhouses? Because it's fun! Watching a mating pair build a nest, hatch and raise their young offer a wonderful lesson in nature for young and old alike. I loved nothing better than to watch the Phoebes grow, mature and fly. Bluebirds nesting in boxes along the fence of my vegetable garden offered countless pleasurable moments too as we watched the babies take their first peek at the world. Birds can and will adapt to their natural environment, but adding a birdhouse helps them and us by providing additional nesting sites.

Types of Birdhouses

Fancy birdhouses that look like cathedrals or Victorian cottages may please us but birds don't particularly care what the outside of their house looks like. They're attracted to houses that meet their needs for nesting sites. In the wild, birds choose a variety of nesting sites and construct nests using mud, twigs, leaves, sticks, animal hair and many other objects. If you provide birds with a house appealing to them, they'll move in and raise their young. It's thrilling to watch parent birds raise babies. Armed with a pair of binoculars, the home bird enthusiast can enjoy the antics of the growing family and watch the young take their first tentative flaps into the world. It's a great learning experience for children, too.

Because birds select houses based on their shape, size and other factors, if you're considering adding birdhouses to the garden, think about the type of bird you're trying to court.

Some birds adapt to other types of houses. Sparrows, for instance, can move in on the coveted bluebird house, evicting the tenants and raising their own young on last year's bluebird nests.

Backyard gardeners eager to add birdhouses to the yard can add a plain square house with a slanted roof and a nice little opening and hope for the best. Or, read about the specific requirements for each of the five common birds listed below, and select a house to attract a bird that lives in your area. You can purchase ready-made houses at garden centers or kits online. Plans allow woodworkers to construct their own, and many homeowners use scraps of wood from other projects to create birdhouses.

Purple Martin Houses

Purple martins are migratory birds, traveling in large flocks called colonies. They nest in colonies, too. A suitable birdhouse for purple martins actually looks more like an apartment building than a single house. Most purple martin houses consist of large, rectangular birdhouses with multiple tiers and entry holes placed on top of a pole in the middle of a field or lawn. Purple martins winging their way to their nest swoop down and eat insects from the lawn, making them popular garden birds. When purchasing purple martin houses, look for ones with stoppers or plugs that fit into the nesting holes. Purple martins leave the birdhouse to migrate south during the winter, and other species of birds can move into their homes and take over. Use the plugs after the martins have left to reduce the chance of other birds 'squatting' on their birdhouse.

Bluebird Houses

Bluebirds offer bright colors, sweet songs, and great insect eating potential. Their numbers have dwindled due to urbanization. Bluebirds need fields near woods, areas in short supply in cities and suburbs. Those living in rural areas often place bluebird houses on fence posts and field posts to offer a hospitable welcome to their cheery visitors. In return, a bluebird family easily consumes plenty of insects as it feeds and raises its young.

Bluebird house are often constructed of cedar, a tough, durable wood, although pine may be used as long as it is untreated. In the eastern portion of the United States, many bluebird houses feature oval-shaped entrance holes to keep starlings from entering, while western and mountain bluebird houses have round openings. Round may be used in the east too, but be on the lookout for starlings and sparrows; they're notorious for stealing bluebird houses for their own purposes.

Bluebird houses have a long back that extends up and down from the main house. This enables the house to be mounted flush against a tree trunk or fence post. They should not have perches, since bluebirds do not need them. Better houses have a hatch on the side or top that enables easy cleaning. It's recommended that you open the bluebird houses in the fall and clean out the old nesting materials. Bluebird houses not only attract other birds, they're also attractive to mice and rodents if the nesting materials are left inside; it provides snug winter quarters for rodents, but they may damage or harm the birds or their eggs if the birds return the following spring before the rodents have moved on. For the birds' safety, clean out the bluebird house.

House Wrens

House wrens need small, snug houses, and they prefer them near shrubs or on trees very near shrubs. They want to feel safe and secure. Look for a birdhouse approximately 4 to6" square all around and place it about 5 to 10 feet off the ground in a tree, hedge or tall shrub. The entrance hole should be near the very top of the birdhouse. Most house wren birdhouses are constructed of wood.

Finches

Birdhouses constructed for finches need to be secure against predators. Other bird species such as sparrows, raccoons and other animals love to get into finch nests and steal the eggs or young. A good finch house is made from untreated, durable wood. Finch houses are usually 6" x 6", with a small hole about 1 ¼" in diameter placed about 4 inches from the ground. A slight overhanging roof keeps rain out of their house, and small holes drilled in the four corners of the floor allow for drainage. Place finch houses in trees away from bird feeders and near some screening plants for privacy.

Generic Birdhouses

If you're just getting started attracting wild birds to the garden, choose a plain birdhouse made from untreated wood. Most of the birdhouses featured at the local home and garden big box retailers are suitable for sparrows, finches, and similar small birds, and if you're not fussy about the type of bird you attract, they're fine and offer enticing potential for nesting pairs. Hang the birdhouse in a tree that offers protection. An area of the yard with mixed terrain such as a bit of lawn leading up to a tree with a few hedges, shrubs or rose bushes nearby is ideal. Each of these plants provides the birds with places to eat, hide and perch, and offers them the feeling of security they crave.

Chapter Five: Diseases, Pests and Predators

It's an unfortunate aspect of a backyard bird feeding hobby that feeding the birds can create problems. While feeding wild birds doesn't create dependency in birds (they can still find their own food if for some reason you stop feeding them), diseases can be spread through dirty feeders and birdbaths. Bird feeders attract other creatures eager for seeds such as squirrels and mice that can quickly become a nuisance and eat more seed than the birds. Anywhere birds congregate, predators congregate too, from your pet cat looking for some fun to local wildlife eager for a quick meal. Here's how to prevent the spread of bird diseases[iii], take steps to ward off other animals eager to eat the bird's food, and prevent predators from harming wild birds.

Preventing the Spread of Diseases

Sickness strikes birds in the wild, and seeing a sick bird at your bird feeder doesn't necessarily mean it got sick at your particular feeder. Remember that some birds travel far distances for food, water and shelter, and they don't care about backyards, property lines and fences. That said, if you see a sick bird, you need to take precautions to prevent it from spreading its illness to other birds.

What does a sick wild bird look like? It may be huddled up near the feeder and appear listless. If you watch for a while, it might not fly away or fly around as much as the other birds. They may cower or hop way from other birds.

Numerous protozoa, bacteria and mold can make birds sick ranging from salmonella to Aspergillosis, a mold that often grows on old bird seed or seed dropped to the ground. To prevent diseases from appearing and spreading from your bird feeder, the Oregon County Cooperative Extension Office[iv] recommends taking the following steps:

Give birds plenty of space. Too many birds on one feeder puts them in closer contact with one another than they might be in the wild, making it easy for them to spread disease. Consider hanging a second feeder.

Keep the feeder clean. Both the National Wildlife Health Center and the Oregon State County Cooperative Extension office recommend cleaning and disinfecting bird feeders monthly in a bleach and water solution. Use 1 part chlorine bleach to 9 parts warm water, rinse with this solution, then rinse with clean plain water and allow the feeder to air dry.

Keep birdseed dry. Wet birdseed creates moist conditions that encourage the growth of molds and fungi that can harm birds. Store birdseed in airtight containers in dry areas. Discard the seed if you see mold or if takes on a peculiar odor.

Discard broken feeders. Squirrels nibble on the edges of bird feeders to widen the holes so that more seeds spill out. Birds such as grackles often do the same, pecking plastic openings larger. This may create jagged edges that can cut birds' feet and legs. Such wounds can become infected. Discard feeders that have been gnawed or chewed by predators.

Clean birdbaths. Scrub and rinse birdbaths weekly, keeping them clear of algae and droppings.

Taking these steps can help wild birds prosper but they're not guarantee that all birds seen in your yard remain healthy. You may want to find the phone number of the local bird sanctuary or wildlife refuge. Contact them if you think you've spotted a sick bird and ask for advice.

Outwitting Squirrels

One evening I saw a television special about squirrels on a nature program in which a scientist tested their memory and problem solving abilities. He placed squirrels at the start of an obstacle course and peanuts at the end. The obstacles forced the squirrels to open latches and doors, move levers and do all sorts of things before proceeding on to the next obstacle. The scientist noted how many obstacles he could put in front of the squirrel before it gave up or forgot how to overcome each obstacle. The squirrel had to remember the task it faced the last time it ran the obstacle course in order to reach the next obstacle in the series. The scientist was astonished when the squirrels he studied could easily remember 24 to 26 tasks in order to reach their peanuts!

This goes to show that squirrels are creative, clever creatures bent on securing food for themselves – and bird feeders provide the equivalent of an all you can eat buffer. Many articles, tales, gadgets and gizmos have tried to thwart the stubborn squirrel from reaching the birdseed in the feeder. Some work better than others.

There are bird feeders available on the market with so-called squirrel baffles on them. These are clear, umbrella-shaped domes that rest over the top of the bird feeder. Such feeders are hung on long chains from trees. Birds can fly to the perches or openings and reach the seed, but squirrels descending from the tree down the chain cannot reach the feed. Once on the dome-shaped baffle, as they lean over they tip the feeder and spill off.

I have seen some that worked and some that had the Albert Einstein of squirrels figure out how to hang by his toes and reach under for feed. You can try them but don't be disappointed if the squirrel wins!

The best squirrel baffles I've seen have been used on pole-mounted feeders. Pole mounted feeders use a thick metal pole stuck into the ground with a platform and tube feeder on top. As long as there are no trees nearby from which squirrels can jump and reach the platform, such feeders deter many squirrels. As squirrels shimmy up the pole, they find they can't easily reach up and over the platform; their feet slip on the metal. Greasing the pole with petroleum jelly or a similar substance also slides them right off.

The most ingenious device I've ever seen was a bird feeder with shutters that closed when the squirrels landed on the feeder. The spring that triggered the shutters to snap shut was balanced by weight, so that lightweight little birds kept it open while heavier squirrels forced it closed.

Sometimes you just have to live with squirrels. I've found that rotating the location of my feeders helps, as does taking the seed feeders down in the summer. Rotating the location of the feeders makes it harder for the squirrels to find them the next year. Taking them down for several months also discourages those who've come to rely upon the bird feeder as an all-you-can-eat banquet.

Mice, rats and other rodents may also be attracted to the feeder. This is a little tougher and my best advice is to just take down the feeder for a while. Although you have to sacrifice your bird watching hobby for a few weeks, this will give the rodents time to get the hint that their easy source of food has vanished and they need to move on. Never use poisons or other chemical repellants; these can kill birds as easily as they kill rodents.

Cats and Predators

It's sad but true. Our beloved pet cats love nothing more than to chase and capture birds. Other predators too find that bird feeders are like watering holes, bringing large flocks of birds within close proximity.

You can keep your own pet cat inside or provide it with a collar and bell to warn the birds. Feral cats and neighbors' cats provide additional problems. You can't keep them indoors nor can you bell them. The trick is to repel them!

Citrus oil is an organic spray oil made from citrus fruits with a pungent scent cats hate. Most humans find the smell pleasant or innocuous, and birds aren't affected by it.

Other things you can do to keep cats and wild predators from harming birds at your bird feeder include:

Hanging feeders 10 feet away from bushes and shrubs. Bushes and shrubs provide screening and cover for predators, who lie in wait before pouncing on the birds. The 10 foot perimeter gives the birds enough time to (hopefully) get out of the way of a charging cat or other wild predator and fly away.

Placing chicken wire or branches with thorns in a box shape near the foot of a bird feeder pole or under a bird feeder. The wire or thorns discourage cats and predators such as raccoons.

Dogs are great for scaring cats and predators away. They usually won't harm birds.

If your cat does snag a bird, don't be too hard on Puss. It's his natural instincts kicking in. Try the bell on the collar and other methods for keeping him away from the feeders. Cats and birds never mixed well in the wild, and now both are in a domestic setting in the yard. It's going to be a while before these sworn enemies ever call a truce.

Chapter Six: Bird Watching Activities and Crafts

I hope that you've taken the first steps to attracting wild birds to the garden and have placed a feeder, started some organic gardening practices, and perhaps planted a tree or shrub that encourages visits from wild birds. As your interest in wild birds grows, perhaps your children (if you have any) will become interested, too. One way you can encourage bird feeding and bird watching as a family activity is to engage children through crafts, activities and interests.

Bird Watching

Serious birdwatchers travel far and wide to seek new species to observe in the wild. You don't need to travel outside of the comfort of your home or backyard to start a bird watching hobby. All you need is a good bird identification guide, a notebook (or the enclosed log sheet), a feeder to attract birds, and a keen eye. A pair of field glasses or binoculars aids in bird identification by magnifying the details on the wild birds; some species appear identical save for fine details such as small bits of color near the eyes, certain wing feathers, or bill shape. Using binoculars to focus on specific features helps novices narrow down the potential species for their new bird friend.

My favorite field guide is the old standby- the *Peterson's Field Guide to Birds*. I have both the Peterson's Guide and the Audubon Guide, which are both good, but I turn to Peterson's time and time again. The first time you use a bird field guide you may be confused. Each guide lists birds different; most cluster similar species together, which as you get used to the guide, you'll begin to understand makes a lot of sense. For example, when the small gray-brown birds began building their nest on our ceiling fan on the front porch, I ran to the Peterson's guide for identification assistance since I didn't recognize their species on sight. I was trying to choose between two species. The photographs in the Peterson's book looked identical. The final clue that identified the nesting pair as Phoebes was a small distinguishing factor. Phoebes bob their tails up and down while perching or singing. Our two little nesters certainly bobbed vigorously as they perches on the roof, convincing me we had two wonderful Phoebes.

The easiest way I have found to teach newcomers to identify birds is to start with what they know and work from there. Do you know how to recognize any bird species? Cardinals, with their bright red feathers, are perhaps one of the easiest birds to identify in the wild. In the northeast where I grew up and the southeast where I live now, I know of no other bird with bright red feathers like the cardinal. If you know what a cardinal looks like, open your bird book and read about cardinals. Note that the males have the bright red feathers; take a good look at the female. Her feathers are more brownish-red, with red shading. Cardinals mate for life, so chances are if you spot a male, his wife is nearby. Can you find her?

Another common bird most people can identify is the Blue Jay. Again, start with what you know. Do you know their raucous cry? They're easier, in my opinion, to notice in the fall when they vie for acorns; they love oaks and other nut trees, and you'll hear their loud screech as they flock to the trees.

Other birds most novices can identify are mourning doves. These are often found in pairs gently pecking at the ground under bird feeders. Sparrows, grackles, crows, and perhaps finches round out the easiest birds to identify.

From there, work on learning a bit about how to identify birds. The things to note when you spot an unusual bird at the feeder are:

Color – what is the bird's primary plumage color?

Markings – does he have certain markings on the wings, head or near the eyes, the most common places where bird species color varies?

Bill shape – long and narrow? Pointy?

Size

Feeding habit – is he on the ground pecking at seeds or up in the feeder? On the trunk of a tree or swooping through the air and snapping up insects?

After purchasing a bird field guide, flip through it and get to know how it's arranged. Look at the color photographs and note the habitat maps. Most bird books have colorized maps that show where certain species live. Obviously if you live in the high desert areas of the southwest, the birds visiting your yard will be different than someone living in Cape Cod. While some birds live throughout the entire United States, many have specific territories they live in. Others migrate, so you might see new and unusual birds in the spring and fall "just passing through" on their way to their nesting and summer quarters.

You can also keep a small notebook and a pencil near your favorite bird watching window. Mornings and late afternoon are the best time to observe birds, by the way. That's when many birds choose to feed, so you may want to visit your "bird watching post" at those times, taking your log book with you.

Photography

The photos in this book were taken by amateur photographers throughout the United States and posted to Morguefile, a file sharing website that allows reproduction of images. Many people love taking photographs of birds, and combining your artistic talent with bird watching can be a natural match. You may want to invest in a telephoto lens and a tripod to steady the camera while taking bird photographs. Hummingbirds whir by so quickly that you may need to adjust the settings on your camera to capture them.

Bird Feeding Crafts

In addition to making your own birdseed blends as noted in the chapter on bird feeding, you can make your own suet feeder. This is a great craft to do with children and although it's messy and a bit sticky, it's a good wintertime project.

Pinecone Suet Feeder

You will need:

Large pinecone

Wire or string

Smooth peanut butter

Birdseed

Spread newspaper on your work table. Place a tablespoon of peanut butter on a plate. Roll the pinecone in the peanut butter or use a knife to spread it on the sides of the pinecone. Place birdseed on a plate and roll the coated pinecone in the seed. Seed should stick to the peanut butter. Tie the wire or string around the pinecone near the top and leave a long length to hang it from the tree. Hang it and enjoy!

Make a Mesh Suet Feeder

You can also make a hanging suet feeder using items that would normally end up in the garbage. Save the wire mesh bags used to package onions or grapefruit. If you eat bacon, fry it on the stovetop and pour off the drippings into a heat proof container, storing the bacon fat in the refrigerator and adding to it over time until you have enough to form a ball the size of a baseball. When you have enough fat, spread some newspaper and have rags or paper towels handy while you make your suet feeder (it's messy and you'll want to wipe your hands frequently). Form the bacon fat into a ball the size of a baseball and roll into a cup of birdseed, pressing the seed in on all sides. You can add raisins or shelled peanuts too if you wish. Place the suet ball into the mesh bag, close it off with string and trim away the excess mesh. Hang on a tree and you have a homemade suet feeder. When the suet is gone, throw away the bag.

Making Birdhouses and Bird Feeders

Birdhouse kits abound, and many craft stores, home and garden centers and specialty stores sell them. There are books and plans to make all sorts of birdhouses and feeders from the simple to the elaborate. For those who enjoy woodworking and crafts, purchasing and making a kit offers an additional outlet for your hobby. Children can make a simple birdhouse with adult supervision and many Scout troops make birdhouses as part of their programs.

Attracting Wild Birds to the Garden: Summary

I hope you've enjoyed this book on attracting wild birds to the garden. Remember, the steps to attracting birds include:

Providing a feeder suitable to the birds you want to attract

Serving up feed that meets their dietary needs

Offering places nearby to perch and hide (shrubs and trees)

Planting trees, shrubs and flowers conducive to birds

Adding a simple water feature, if possible, such as a birdbath

Using organic gardening practices to support all the wildlife in the local ecosystem

Storing birdseed in a dry location away from mice and other critters

Cleaning feeders, birdhouses and birdbaths regularly to prevent the spread of disease

Keeping domestic cats and other predators away from feeders or making it difficult for them to stalk and kill wild birds

And to enhance your enjoyment of backyard birds...

Purchase and use a good birding field guide to identify species.

Add birdhouses to observe nesting behavior and baby birds.

Make crafts such as suet feeders or birdhouses.

Bird Watching for Life

Remember these words of wisdom from another gardener:

"I value my garden more for being full of blackbirds than of cherries" –
Joseph Addison (1672-1719)

In today's busy world, with all the modern entertainments vying for our attention, taking time to stop and smell the roses – or listen and watch the birds – helps us reconnect with the natural world and nurtures us body, mind and soul. Take a moment to observe and feed the birds. Breathe. Relax. Enjoy!

Resources for Bird Watching and Identification

Cornell University Laboratory of Ornithology offers audio clips to help you identify birds by song and much, much more. http://www.birds.cornell.edu

What Birds offers a free online bird identification guide. There's even an iBird app you can download to your phone for portable bird identification. http://www.whatbird.com

National Bird Feeding Society, http://www.birdfeeding.org

National Audubon Society, http://www.audubon.org

Project Feeder Watch – bird feeding and birding resources - http://www.birds.cornell.edu/pfw/AboutBirdsandFeeding/abtbirds_index.html

Bird Identification Books

Peterson, Roger Tory. *Petersons Field Guide to Birds of North America*, Sixth Edition.

Robbins, Chandler. *Guide to Field Identification of Birds of North America*.

How to Attract Birds. Ortho Books.

About the Author

Jeanne Grunert is an award-winning writer and content marketer living and working on a 17 acre farm in Virginia. Prior to moving to Virginia in 2007, Jeanne led the marketing department for a variety of publishing and education companies in the New York City area. Today, she grows a life instead of just making a living. She is the author of *Pricing Your Services - 21 Tips for More Profit* and *An Ancient Gift and Other Stories*, available on Amazon.com and Smashwords.com, and blogs about her exploits at Seven Oaks, her farm, at www.homegardenjoy.com.

Other Books by Jeanne Grunert

Available from Smashwords.com, Amazon.com or wherever ebooks are sold.

Pricing Your Services: 21 Tips for More Profit

An Ancient Gift and Other Stories

Connect with Jeanne Grunert

Email: jeannegrunert@gmail.com
Company Website: www.marketing-writer.com

Home Garden Joy: www.homegardenjoy.com

Facebook: https://www.facebook.com/sevenoaksgardening

Twitter: @jeannegrunert

REFERENCES AND CITATION in the text

i

      "Does Winter Bird Feeding Promote Dependence?" Department of Wildlife publication, University of Wisconsin. Citation from 1988 U.S. Fish and Wildlife. Accessed at: http://www.johnstoncc.edu/howellwoods/DisplayReading.aspx?PDFID=5

ii   "Garden bird feeding predicts the structure of avian assemblages." Richard A. Fuller, Philip H. Warren, Paul R. Armsworth, Olga Barbosa, Kevin J. Gaston. *Diversity and Distributions*, Volume 14, Issue 1, pages 131-137, January 2008. Abstract accessed at

http://onlinelibrary.wiley.com/doi/10.1111/j.1472-4642.2007.00439.x/abstract;jsessionid=4C60D231793B85284E7A061E27DA78B6.d03t01

iii   U.S. Department of the Interior, National Wildlife Health Center, free publication,
http://www.nwhc.usgs.gov/publications/fact_sheets/coping_with_diseases_at_birdfeeders.jsp

iv   Extension Service Garden Hints,
http://extension.oregonstate.edu/news/story.php?S_No=848&storyType=garde

Printed in Great Britain
by Amazon